"Awake in a dream, walking between worlds"
Aimee Traeden

Published by Ulv Bjørn Press
ISBN Paperback: 979-8-9991505-0-9
ISBN Hardback: 979-8-9991505-1-6
ISBN Digital: 979-8-9991505-2-3

Cover design and illustrations by Aimee Traeden, combining digital creation and hand-guided adaptation.
Printed in United States of America
First Edition

THE GRIEF TREE

SACRED INITIATION THROUGH LOSS AND TRANSFORMATION

Written by Aimee Traeden

THE WISDOM TREES
BOOK ONE

This is my gift to you from one griever's heart to another.

And to Rick Bateman, whose loss carried me through the deepest
ocean of grief I have ever known, I miss you and love you forever.

The Journey

Introduction

Grief is not merely an emotion, it is a landscape we will all journey through in our lives. An inevitable, transformative initiation, it reshapes us in ways we never expected. The Grief Tree is the first book in The Wisdom Trees series, a collection of stories woven from my personal relationship with the natural world, non-ordinary reality, myth, mysticism, and magick. Guided by my deep connection to my ancient ancestors, each book explores the depths of soul through a different emotion, drawing from my experiences traversing the shamanic realms and the wisdom revealed to me through the standing ones, the Trees.

This is not a roadmap out of grief, nor a guide to mastering loss. It is an invitation to step into a relationship with sorrow, to witness its wisdom, and to allow it to transform you. Through story, reflection, and the language of the unseen, this book offers a way to meet grief with reverence, to find meaning in its presence, and to move with it rather than against it.

If these words resonate, may they serve as a light in the darkness, a companion in the unknown, and a reminder that even in our deepest sorrow, we are never truly alone. May the roots of The Grief Tree remind you that even in sorrow, there is connection. May its branches remind you that grief, like all things, belongs to the great cycle of life. And may the myth and magick held within these pages reveal that grief is not an ending, but a doorway to something deeper.

This is the story of how an Ancient Grandmother Tree shared her deepest wisdom with me, merging her own initiation into grief with mine.

Long ago, she stood mighty and steadfast on the banks of a river, her branches reaching toward the cosmos, her roots woven deep into the soil, intertwined with the stones, mycelium, and the whispers of the ancestors. She was the keeper of her kin, the sentinel, and the mother of a land where everything moved in sacred relationship.

Around her, the forest breathed with birdsong and the murmurs of beasts, pulsing to the heartbeat of the Earth herself. Every leaf, drop of water, and shadow sang its part in a vast harmonious orchestra.

In this sacred forest, grief was unknown. There was only the fullness of life.

It is where we all begin, before the losses, before the grief: unaware of the inevitable changes that will someday come.

One day, the changes began. Grandmother Tree felt them. Beneath her aging bark, tiny movements stirred, a faint crawling, an itch she could not reach. Though she didn't fully understand, she sensed this was the beginning of an ending.

The pine beetles were unseen invaders, small but relentless. Confusion and anger rippled through the Tree, but she knew these beings were also part of the forest, part of the Earth, part of the intricate web of life. So, she stood strong, steadfast in her place. Yet, she could not ignore the undeniable truth: her fortress of thick, beautiful bark was being breached. Something fundamental had shifted. The new sensations brought a strange, foreign awareness, an inevitable knowing that nothing would ever be the same.

Around her, the forest carried on, oblivious to the quiet destruction. Birds still sang, the river still laughed, and the beasts yipped and howled in their daily rhythm. But within the Tree, there was a gnawing awareness of vulnerability. And with it came something else: a strange, new isolation.

I have felt this too. The first whispers when the doorway cracks open, the moment a path to grief reveals itself. Like the beetles, it begins as a slow, uncomfortable creeping into the edges of your soul. You don't yet know what is happening, only that something is unraveling. Something is being lost. Yet, at the same time, something is opening. There is an expansion, a creation of space, space that leads to the unknown, to an entry point into the great mystery.

Everything was moving faster now. The beetles had multiplied, and their hum grew steadily louder. Chewing their way through her trunk, the beetles carved intricate pathways, a mysterious new language etched into her very being. Staying as she was became impossible. Parts of her swayed and weakened; where once her heart had been shielded, it now bore holes that weakened her defenses, and her branches began to sag under the weight of decay.

She could no longer fight the inevitable. One day, with a thunderous crash that reverberated through the forest, a massive branch gave way, tumbling through the air before landing with a resounding splash in the river below.

The water embraced her fallen limb, as gently as a mother catching her child, and carried it downstream. The Wise Grandmother powerlessly watched it go. This was the gateway where denial shatters and grief takes root.

I remember when my own branches fell, when I realized I could no longer hold what I loved. The portal to grief is not merely a doorway; it feels like a destabilizing collapse, a surrender to the current, drawing you deeper into the unknown.

The branch's journey down the river mirrored my own. It tumbled through rapids, battered and bruised, each collision stripping it bare. This was the chaos of early grief, relentless, unpredictable currents that leave you gasping for breath.

Then came the calm stretches, moments when the river cradled the branch gently and the surface reflected the wide-open sky. In these still waters, time seemed to slow, allowing space to notice the shifting landscape: new birds calling overhead, broad-leafed Maples lining the banks, and playful new creatures wading in the shallows. These brief respites brought gratitude and a deep appreciation for life's beauty, softening the fear of what lay ahead.

Such moments were like the times when I could finally breathe. When the tears paused and a faint flicker of peace broke through. Hope would wash over me, settling my turmoil just enough to reveal the beauty beneath the loss, a place of appreciation for what had been, and for what could still be.

One quiet day, the branch drifted ashore, resting among stones and debris. For a time, it lay unnoticed until a curious traveler came upon it. Entranced by the intricate writing left by the beetles, she ran her fingers along its mysteriously etched surface. In that moment, the branch found a new purpose, to support this traveler on her journey, steadying each step as she climbed treacherous mountain paths and navigated steep descents. No longer weak or sickly, the branch stood strong and capable in its separation from the Tree.

When her travels ended, the traveler chose to return the branch to the forest's edge rather than keep it, placing it gently among the roots and fallen leaves. There, the limb lay in quiet reflection, integrating its new sense of identity, an individuation born from separation and shaped by its experiences.

Then, a sudden gust of wind swept the branch back into the river. Its journey was far from over; a new one had begun.

Grief, too, never truly ends. It flows, transforms, and carries us onward, revealing new perspectives in its wake. I have been that branch, molded by grief, transformed into something unexpected, and carried by the support of others. And I have been the traveler, finding strength in what once was broken and offering it new life.

After several more days of floating, the river gave way to the ocean, vast and boundless, dissolving into endless blue. The branch floated into this expanse, a mere speck in an immeasurable sea. But this was unlike the river: no banks, no predictable flow, only swirling currents pulling in every direction. This was grief fully expanded, a realm where all emotions coexist, sorrow and despair, anger and rage, joy and love, all flowing together, indistinguishable yet whole.

I have stood at the edge of this ocean, overwhelmed by its magnitude, and I have been carried by its waves. I have learned that to grieve is to surrender to the tides: to let yourself be carried without knowing your destination, to allow the waves to draw you deep into the unknown, then bring you back to the surface beneath a sparkling night sky and glowing moon, only to repeat the cycle. These tides have taught me to go with rather than resist, to dive without fear, trusting that the current will eventually return me to the surface, to the lightness of being once more.

Time passed, and soon the branch came to a place of quiet contentment, as it integrated its journey in the calmer waters that now gently rocked it. For a time, it rested in peace. But before long, the branch sensed a stirring beneath the waves, a powerful presence. It was the Goddess of the deep waters, the keeper of every emotion within the vast landscape of grief.

The Goddess recognized the branch and the magic wisdom it carried from the Grandmother Tree, so she plucked it from the sea. Carrying it as a staff, she made her way toward the shore, where a woman sat watching the sunset.

That woman was me.

I was broken by losses too numerous to name. I had witnessed my world collapse, my branches fall. I had tumbled through rapids and drifted through calm waters. I had been carried and leaned upon, just as I had carried others. I had passed from the river into the darkest depths of the ocean. Now, I sat at the edge of it all, gazing silently at the horizon, wondering why.

Then I saw her—luminous, shifting like the tide, her eyes reflecting the weight of every tear ever shed. She rose from the waters, bearing the branch in her hands, etched with mysterious markings.

The sea goddess approached, radiating both tenderness and strength. Holding the branch like a mighty staff in one hand, she reached out with the other, lifting me from the shoreline. Her gaze met mine, piercing straight into the edges of my soul.

She leaned in and whispered, "Grief is your gift, my darling. It is not a curse or a burden. It connects you to the mystery of life itself. It is the very essence of soul. It is the missing piece that has guided you to compassion and tenderness. Grief is the answer you seek." With these words, she placed the branch in my hands.

In that instant, something ineffable occurred. I felt the story of the Wise Grandmother Tree flow into me—the loss of her branch, and the branch's entire journey. The markings on the wood glowed, threads of light radiating into my being. I saw the landscapes of grief, not as stages to fix or overcome, but as a vast tapestry of emotions, anger, despair, joy, fear, shock, denial, gratitude, stillness, and love, all woven into the fabric of life.

I wept then, not solely from sorrow, but with profound gratitude. In that moment, the fissure in my heart expanded so wide grief showed me how it had shaped me, softened my edges, and opened me to a love so profound it could not be contained. This was wholeness. It was the very definition of existence.

Suddenly, I was back in my body, staring into the eyes of that magnificent being. She smiled softly, then turned away, returning to the ocean until her luminous form melted into the waves. She left me with the branch, a sturdy staff, a reminder, a gift. I no longer felt burdened, but transformed. And so I began my walk along the shore.

As the sun began to dip below the horizon, I stood in deep reverence, fully aware that grief never truly ends. It is both a beginning and a path we all must take, a journey through a landscape, leading us into the deepest parts of our souls.

Grief is a gift, a thread connecting us to what has been lost and to the love that endures. It weaves us into the web that interconnects us all, an intricate entanglement of truth and undeniable growth. Though this journey is seldom easy, it is sacred and is uniquely ours.

The End

Acknowledgements

Thank you to Grief, both the weight and the wisdom, for being one of my greatest teachers.

Thank you to everyone who has ever supported me through my own pain and losses, too many to count.

◊ To Mindy Corral, for the countless times you answered the phone and listened to me snot cry on the floor, no matter what.

◊ To Raina Corah, for offering me unwavering support without conditions, always reminding me that I am seen and loved exactly as I am.

◊ To my mom, Ellen Michals, who has been reading and listening to my never-ending stories since the moment I could speak. Your patience, love, and encouragement have carried me through my life. You are the greatest, most magical Mom one could have ever hoped for.

◊ To my dad, Jens Traeden, who may have grown tired of my stories but always cherished my creative soul. Your pride in my imagination gave me the courage to keep dreaming.

◊ To the Spirits of Grief and the Branch that entered my life and led me on this journey, you changed my understanding of loss in ways I never could have foreseen. You taught me that grief is not just sorrow, but transformation.

◊ And to Erin Donley, for keeping me motivated, for reminding me that my words matter, and for pushing me to see this through. Without your encouragement, this book might still be a whisper instead of a reality.

With deepest gratitude,
Aimee

Lady of The Wolves

Aimee Traeden is a mystic, a shamanic practitioner devoted to ancestral wisdom, sacred rites, and soul transformation. As a seer and storyteller, she walks the in-between, guiding others through the initiatory thresholds of death, grief, and becoming.

Rooted in her Nordic and Celtic lineages, Aimee's work weaves shamanic journeying, sound healing, and ritual with deep reverence for the unseen. With an intimate, lifelong bond to the spirit world, she channels ancestral voices and holds space for profound healing.

She is the light between both darknesses, the deep of the earth and the silence of the stars. A thread between death and rebirth. A witness to the unraveling and the rising.

As the creator of The Wisdom Trees series, Aimee distills myth, memory, and medicine into evocative stories that honor grief as a sacred gift, a force that reshapes, deepens, and connects us to what matters most.

When she's not writing, she expresses her artistry through painting, music, and talismanic objects and jewelry. She lives in Utah, with her husband and three beloved dogs, held by the mountains and the wild spirit of the land.

Find her at: www.aimeetraeden.com
Instagram @aimeetraeden